A Gift For:

From:

Published by Hallmark Gift Books,
a division of Hallmark Cards, Inc.,
Kansas City, MO 64141
Visit us on the Web at Hallmark.com.

Editorial Director: Delia Berrigan
Editor: Kara Goodier
Art Director: Chris Opheim
Designer: Scott Swanson
Production Designer: Dan Horton
Contributing Writers: Ellen Brenneman,
Megan Haave, Tom Shay-Zapien, Drew Wagner,
Molly Wigand, and Melvina Young

ISBN 978-1-63059-974-4
BOK2252

Made in China
0518

ADVICE
FOR
MY SON

EVEN THE WORST DAY CAN'T LAST MORE THAN 24 HOURS.

LIFE ISN'T ABOUT HAVING THE RIGHT ANSWERS. IT'S ABOUT ASKING THE RIGHT QUESTIONS.

NEVER TEXT IN ANGER.

WRAP YOUR ARMS AROUND SOMETHING OR SOMEONE YOU LOVE. A TREE, A BOOK, A PERSON, A CHEESEBURGER . . . NOTE: IF IT'S A CHEESEBURGER, USE YOUR HANDS INSTEAD.

DON'T PLAY TO WIN. JUST PLAY TO PLAY.

> **SAVE THINGS THAT MATTER. PITCH THE REST. THE EASIEST RULE TO KEEP LIFE SIMPLE: SURROUND YOURSELF WITH THINGS THAT BRING YOU JOY.**

WRITE A LETTER TO SOMEONE.

KEEP THE OWNER'S MANUAL. It holds the answers to many of the little issues you may have with a product. And if it doesn't, sometimes there's a warranty you didn't know about in the back.

HAVE ONE SPECIAL FOOD. THEN NEVER HAVE IT.

SAVE IT FOR SPECIAL OCCASIONS AND PICK-ME-UPS.

TAKE A FEW STEPS BACK AND SEE THE BIGGER PICTURE.

YOU GET WHAT YOU PAY FOR.

Some things you should never buy cheap: paint and paintbrushes, tools, lawn mowers, mattresses, and pots and pans.

....

PRINT IMPORTANT THINGS.

....

CHECK YOUR TIRE PRESSURE BEFORE A ROAD TRIP. OR ANY LONGER-THAN-USUAL DRIVE.

....

SAY YES TO THE WORLD. That adventure you've wanted to go on? That place you really want to see? Plan it out. Make it happen.

DON'T PLAY BALL IN THE HOUSE.
NOT BECAUSE YOU'LL BREAK SOMETHING, BUT BECAUSE THERE IS LITERALLY A WHOLE WORLD OUT THERE TO PLAY IN.

TEN PERCENT OF ALL PAYCHECKS SHOULD GO INTO SAVINGS. IT'S ALWAYS GOOD TO HAVE A LITTLE NEST EGG IN CASE OF EMERGENCIES.

WEAR A HELMET.

IF YOU CAN'T FIX IT YOURSELF, YOU MIGHT AS WELL MAKE IT WORTH THE TECHNICIAN'S TIME. If something breaks, and it's definitely broken, why not see if you can fix it yourself? As long as it has nothing to do with plumbing or electricity. Or anything else that can kill you or destroy your home.

DON'T TOUCH YOUR FACE WITH YOUR HANDS.

YOU DON'T WANT ALL THOSE OILS AND GERMS ON YOUR HANDSOME FACE.

DON'T DRIVE INTO STANDING WATER.

It can carry you away faster than you can even imagine. The same is true for thinking you can tempt fate with other risky decisions. Some guys make it through to the other side, and some guys don't.

NO MATTER WHAT YOU'RE LOOKING FOR, YOU'LL ALWAYS FIND IT. BLESSINGS. BAD THINGS. GOOD THINGS. KEEP YOUR EYES OPEN TO THEM ALL.

IF YOU SEE INJUSTICE HAPPENING, STEP IN.

ADVERTISING ISN'T REAL. No one product will make your life perfect or guarantee your happiness. In reality, you're the only one who can make good things happen for you or decide what makes you happy.

EVERY DAY SHOULD BE LIKE A HOT DOG—full of all kinds of weird stuff that makes you happy. Sometimes dumb jokes are part of this stuff.

....

DON'T TAKE YOURSELF TOO SERIOUSLY.

PART OF BEING A GOOD SPORT IS LAUGHING AT YOURSELF.

....

LISTEN TO THE MESSAGE OF THE LEAVES. No day is so bad that a long walk in the woods or by a lake won't make it better. We spent thousands of years making our livings outdoors, and there's still some part of us that wants to get out in nature once in a while.

WAVES MAKE WAVES MAKE WAVES.

Every action we take or word we speak affects others. Take this to heart and think of the consequences you're setting in motion with every decision you make. Remember, with unkind words, less is more. With encouragement, more is more.

ANIMALS ARE GOOD FOR YOUR HEART.

PETTING A DOG OR CAT CAN LOWER STRESS LEVELS. **IT'S SCIENCE.**

GIVE ALL YOU HAVE. ESPECIALLY IF WHAT YOU HAVE IS KINDNESS.

THROW OUT OLD UNDERWEAR YEARLY.

LIVE LIKE YOU'RE SOMEBODY'S HERO. YOU JUST MIGHT BE. CAPE AND TIGHTS OPTIONAL.

IT DOESN'T MATTER WHERE LIFE STARTS. WHAT MATTERS IS WHERE IT GOES BEFORE IT ENDS. YOU'RE WRITING YOUR OWN STORY EACH DAY. HOW DO YOU WANT TO BE REMEMBERED?

YOU CAN NEVER HAVE TOO MUCH COURAGE OR DETERMINATION.

MAKE BOLD CHOICES.

BOLD CHOICES BUILD CHARACTER, AND THIS WORLD COULD USE A FEW MORE CHARACTERS.

FOLD OR HANG YOUR LAUNDRY IMMEDIATELY WHEN IT COMES OUT OF THE DRYER. Then apply this principle to paying bills, cleaning house, mowing the lawn, and any other tasks that grow more imposing and distasteful when you procrastinate.

BE A GOOD HOST.

IF YOU GET UP TO GET A DRINK, OFFER ONE TO YOUR GUESTS AS WELL.

HELP AND GIVE TO OTHERS WITH NO THOUGHT OF RETURN.

WHAT HAPPENS IN OUR LIVES CAN CHANGE US. WHAT WE DO ABOUT IT CAN CHANGE EVERYTHING.

··

DO SOMETHING NICE FOR THE EARTH.

AFTER ALL, SHE'S PRETTY NICE TO YOU EVERY DAY.

··

WHEN OUT IN PUBLIC, DON'T OVERDO THE WHOLE "COMFY CLOTHES" THING. THERE'S NOTHING WRONG WITH SOME GOOD COMFY SWEATPANTS AND SLIPPERS, ESPECIALLY ON THOSE RAINY DAYS INDOORS. BUT WHEN HEADING TO THE STORE OR OUT INTO THE WORLD, MAYBE GRAB THE SWEATS THAT AREN'T TATTERED AND BLEACH-SPOTTED. THAT WAY, IF YOU RUN INTO SOMEONE YOU KNOW—OR MIGHT LIKE TO KNOW—YOU'LL FEEL MORE PRESENTABLE.

··

Courage is the power to let go. Faith is the belief that someone will catch you. It's like when you learned to jump in the pool: At first you depended on me, then your water wings, to help you stay afloat. But eventually you learned that the laws of nature and the world itself will buoy you. It's a sweet metaphor for conquering new fears (and there will be new ones) of every kind.

DON'T WORRY ABOUT TOMORROW.

THE ONLY FUTURE YOU REALLY OWN IS THE MOMENT RIGHT IN FRONT OF YOU. SO QUIT WORRYING. QUIT. WORRYING. BREATHE. BREATHE. COUNT TO TEN. BREATHE.

SEPARATE YOUR COLORED CLOTHES FROM YOUR WHITES. BECAUSE NOTHING MAKES A WHITE T-SHIRT LOOK OLDER AND WORN-OUT FASTER THAN BEING TINTED GREY-BLUE.

WRITE THANK-YOU NOTES.

In a digital age where a text or typed message is more easy and convenient, a handwritten thank-you note means you appreciate the person enough to sit down and write. Your hand may cramp, and your handwriting might not look as good as the default font setting, but the gesture alone means so much more than clicking "SEND."

WHEN LIFE SEEMS HARD, GET AWAY SOMEPLACE WILD.

Build a fire, roast hot dogs and s'mores, and share a few tall tales with your buds. Sleep under the stars and you'll likely come back to the problem with fresh eyes.

DON'T DWELL IN THE PAST.

You're only as good as your last success, and as bad as your last failure. Whatever the outcome of any project, pick yourself up and start planning your next venture. Don't rest on successes for too long and don't let a misstep ruin your forward momentum.

LEARN HOW TO PLAY AN INSTRUMENT.

ON A DATE, ASK 25% MORE **THAN YOU ANSWER.**

GET THREE ESTIMATES WHEN HIRING SOMEONE TO DO WORK. IF IT SEEMS LIKE A BARGAIN, IT MAY NOT BE GOOD QUALITY WORK. WITH DIFFERENT QUOTES, YOU'LL GET A GOOD IDEA OF THE AVERAGE COST WITHOUT BEING OVERCHARGED.

DO KARAOKE. Even if it's just once. And really get into it. There are few times in life when you'll feel the same level of elation and humiliation, only to walk away at the end of it and realize you're just fine.

FIND A SUNNY SPOT. INTRODUCE YOURSELF. SIT WITH IT AWHILE. GO BACK TO IT AS OFTEN AS YOU CAN.

MAKE A LITTLE KID LAUGH.

YOU WON'T HEAR A SWEETER SOUND.

REMEMBER . . . GOOD MANNERS NEVER, EVER GO OUT OF STYLE. YOU'RE WELCOME FOR THE REMINDER.

KEEP AN EXTRA CHANGE OF CLOTHES HANDY—OR AT LEAST AN EXTRA PAIR OF SOCKS.

DO AS I SAY, NOT AS I DO.

UNLESS I SAY SOMETHING STUPID, AND I WILL SAY SOMETHING STUPID. SO WILL YOU WHEN YOU'RE A PARENT. AND THEN YOU SHOULD EXTEND THIS SAME DISCLAIMER TO YOUR KIDS. P.S. SORRY I'M IMPERFECT. **THAT'S LIFE.**

LOOK ON THE BRIGHT SIDE.

SQUINT IF YOU HAVE TO.

DON'T PREOCCUPY YOUR TIME THINKING ABOUT YOUR WEAKNESSES. It may feel like those weaknesses are what others notice, but trust me: They're too busy trying to hide their own insecurities.

NEVER CONFUSE HAVING A TO-DO LIST WITH HAVING A LIFE.

It's easy to get so caught up in daily stuff that you forget the big picture. It may take a bit of figuring out, but find the balance between work stuff, life stuff, and you stuff.

PRACTICE CHANGING A FLAT TIRE ON A DRY, SUNNY DAY. THE WAY LUCK WILL HAVE IT, YOUR FIRST FLAT WILL PROBABLY HAPPEN ON THE SIDE OF THE ROAD DURING A RAINSTORM OR BLIZZARD, AND YOU WON'T WANT TO FIGURE IT OUT AS YOUR FINGERS FREEZE AND YOU GET SOAKED.

FIND YOURSELF THE PERFECT HAT.

VISUALIZE THE LIFE YOU WANT.

Sometimes life lays a freebie in your lap. The best of the best without even trying. Getting a son like you, for instance—that was pure luck. But most of the time, crossing your fingers isn't enough. You have to come up with a plan and keep working at it over the long haul.

GIVE COMPLIMENTS. LIFE IS NOT A COMPETITION, SO TAKE NOTICE OF THE GOOD IN OTHERS. PLUS, A COMPLIMENT IS GUARANTEED TO MAKE THEIR DAY.

Where does your mind wander when you're driving on a quiet road? THAT'S what you should be doing with your life. Don't let life get so hectic that you don't have time to dream, to play what-if, just to be. That's a recipe for waking up at 50 and wondering who you are and what you thought you were doing. Always be sure your life has a mission, and it's one that makes you feel alive.

WORK HARD

BUT NEVER PASS UP A CHANCE TO DANCE.

FILL UP THE TANK AND GO FOR A DRIVE.

TURN UP THE SOUND. ROLL DOWN THE WINDOWS. DO THAT AIRPLANE THINGY WITH YOUR HAND.

THERE ARE SOME THINGS YOU JUST CAN'T CONTROL. **TRY TO BE THE KIND OF PERSON WHO FINDS THIS COMFORTING AND NOT UNBEARABLE.**

FASTEN YOUR SEAT BELT.

IT TAKES SO LITTLE EFFORT TO DO THIS. BUT WHAT THAT LITTLE PIECE OF FABRIC CAN DO IS SO VALUABLE, THERE'S NO REASON NOT TO TAKE THE FIVE SECONDS TO CLIP IT INTO PLACE.

NEVER THROW AWAY ANYTHING YOU WRITE. OR PAINT. OR DRAW. OR WHATEVER CREATIVE PURSUIT YOU LIKE TO EXPLORE. Because once they're gone, they're gone, and looking back on the things you created can be a rewarding—or at least entertaining—experience.

YOU CAN'T RUN FROM YOUR PROBLEMS. Well, you technically can run, but we are all slower than our problems and they will eventually catch up with us. Fortunately, every big problem can be broken down into smaller problems, which in turn can be broken down into even smaller "situations," which can be broken down into more easily solved puzzles. Start there and work your way up.

BACK UP YOUR DIGITAL PHOTOS.

BETTER TO BE OVERDRESSED THAN UNDERDRESSED. WHEN IN DOUBT, WEAR THE TIE AND JACKET. YOU CAN ALWAYS TAKE THEM OFF LATER.

TAKE A MOMENT TO STOP STARING AT YOUR PHONE. SUNRISES AND SUNSETS ARE MUCH BETTER ALTERNATIVES.

FIND BEAUTY IN SMALL THINGS.

TAKE CARE OF YOUR LAWN.

IT MAY SEEM LIKE MORE WORK THAN ITS WORTH, BUT THERE'S NOTHING QUITE LIKE WALKING AROUND BAREFOOT IN YOUR OWN YARD.

IF THINGS GO WRONG, DON'T GO WITH THEM. —ROGER BABSON **"Go with the flow" isn't always the best advice. It's entirely possible to be the only stand-up guy who's in the right, and everyone else is following the herd off a cliff.**

GET TO KNOW YOUR NEIGHBORS. **YOU NEVER KNOW WHEN YOU'LL LOCK YOURSELF OUT OF YOUR PLACE OR NEED SOMEONE TO WATER THE PLANTS.**

IT'S NORMAL TO DISLIKE YOUR FIRST JOB.

Everyone's got to start somewhere. And your first job will more than likely not be the one you've been dreaming about. Just remember: Your first job opens the elevator door, but your work ethic and positive attitude are what get you moving upward.

KEEPING YOUR SOUP BOWL FILLED TO THE BRIM LEAVES YOU WITHOUT ROOM FOR CRACKERS. **THINKING YOU HAVE IT ALL FIGURED OUT IS A GOOD SIGN THAT YOU STILL HAVE MORE TO LEARN.**

EAT WITHOUT SILVERWARE. GIVE YOURSELF A HAND FOR TRYING SOMETHING NEW.

GET ENOUGH SLEEP.

I know you will ignore this advice. But don't blame me tomorrow when you're lurching zombie-like through the daylight hours.

IF YOU DON'T BELIEVE IN YOURSELF, NO ONE ELSE WILL. THERE'LL ALWAYS BE SOMEONE WHO BELIEVES IN YOU— YOUR FAMILY FIRST, LAST, AND ALWAYS. BUT YOU NEED TO BELIEVE IN YOURSELF, AS MUCH OR MORE. ALWAYS RE-MEMBER WHAT STRONG STUFF YOU'RE MADE OF.

GET OUT THERE. GET DIRTY.

A CLEAN UNIFORM MEANS YOU'RE NOT HAVING ENOUGH FUN.

SHARE YOUR FRIES.

OTHER THINGS, TOO.

ALWAYS RETURN THINGS BETTER THAN HOW YOU RECEIVED THEM. Even if it was dirty before you got it, returning something you borrowed in pristine condition makes you look trustworthy and guarantees they'll let you borrow things again.

MAKE "YOU" TIME.

It doesn't matter how busy you are or how hectic things might get, it's always important to make a little time to do the things you love to do. Otherwise, what's the point?

DO YOUR BEST TO MAKE THE MOST OF WHAT YOU HAVE. NO CAMPFIRE? **MICROWAVE THE DANG S'MORES.** NO SHOELACES? **GO BAREFOOT.**

KEEP A COPY OF YOUR FAVORITE MOVIE FROM WHEN YOU WERE LITTLE. WISH THERE WAS A DEEP, PHILOSOPHICAL REASON FOR THIS, BUT THERE'S NOT. BUT THERE'S SOMETHING SPECIAL ABOUT RE-WATCHING IT WHEN YOU'RE OLDER, EITHER BY YOURSELF OR WITH LITTLE ONES OF YOUR OWN.

KEEP A FIRST-AID KIT. THERE'S NOTHING UNMANLY ABOUT PULLING OUT A SPLINTER OR USING SOME STING-RELIEF CREAM.

DON'T FORGET TO LAUGH.

WHEN TIMES ARE GOOD, AND ESPECIALLY WHEN TIMES SEEM BAD.

NEVER SAY NO TO ADVENTURE. OR POPSICLES. There's so little time to be carefree. Savor and make the most of every little minute of fun you can grab. Don't let the responsibilities of growing up keep you from that.

LIFE IS MEANT TO BE GRITTY.

Look for the real people living their real lives with real passion. The shiny and shallow dalliances will compete for your attention, but do not be waylaid. Truth is the North Star, shining in a Big Dipper of integrity and grit.

BE AN HONEST PERSON.

RELIABILITY IS A RARITY. SAY WHAT YOU MEAN, AND STICK TO YOUR WORD.

NEVER UNDERESTIMATE THE POWER OF A GOOD HAIRCUT. SEE ALSO "GROWN-UP SHOES" AND "WELL-FITTING JACKET."

FLY OUT INTO THE WORLD.

IT WAS PROBABLY HARD FOR THE WRIGHT BROTHERS' PARENTS TO WATCH THEIR FIRST FEW BUMBLING EFFORTS AND FALSE STARTS. BUT THAT FEELING THAT THE WORLD IS YOURS FOR THE TAKING? THAT YOU CAN GO AS FAR AS YOU DREAM? ANY PARENT WANTS THAT FOR HIS OR HER CHILD. NO EXCEPTION HERE.

ADULTHOOD REQUIRES A LOT OF HARD WORK AND DEDICATION. COFFEE, DONUTS, AND PIZZA HELP, TOO.

BLANKET FORTS ARE ALWAYS EN VOGUE. THE DAY YOU LOOK AT A BLANKET FORT AND THINK "HOW CHILDISH" IS THE DAY YOU'VE LET GO OF SOMETHING VERY PRECIOUS.

SAY "I'M SORRY."

Some people just say "WHOOPS." Some say "MY BAD." But saying "I'M SORRY" when you make a mistake expresses something more sincere than those other phrases ever could.

BUT DON'T EVER APOLOGIZE FOR BEING EXACTLY WHO YOU ARE.

KEEP YOUR CAR CLEAN. It doesn't matter if you're usually the only one who rides in it. All it takes is one person asking for a ride before you start feeling self-conscious about how messy it is. And you never know if the cop who pulls you over is a neat freak who may deal more harshly with you if the back seat is full of taco wrappers.

HOLD THE DOOR FOR SOMEONE.

IT'S JUST THE POLITE THING TO DO.
AND DO IT FOR EVERYONE.

LOOK LIFE RIGHT IN THE EYE.

GIVE IT A CHALLENGE. YOU CAN TAKE IT.

READ THE NUTRITION INFORMATION ON FOOD. It doesn't matter if the front of the box claims "low-fat" or "healthy." The facts don't lie and will tell you if that's true. If it's one of your favorite snacks, though, maybe don't look at the facts too much. Or at the very least, don't eat that snack too often.

READ BOOKS. I KNOW WHEN YOU'RE YOUNG AND IN SCHOOL THEY MADE YOU READ BOOKS ABOUT THINGS YOU HAD NO INTEREST IN. BUT ONCE YOU GET OUT AND DEVELOP YOUR OWN INTERESTS, IT'S AMAZING HOW MANY BOOKS YOU CAN FIND THAT ARE JUST WHAT YOU'RE LOOKING FOR.

GIVE IT YOUR ALL.

IT SHOWS IN YOUR STANCE, YOUR CARRIAGE, YOUR ENERGY LEVEL, THE SMILE ON YOUR FACE, AND OF COURSE, IN YOUR OUTPUT. IF YOU'RE NOT 100% "THERE" IN WHATEVER YOU'RE TRYING TO DO, IT'S NOTICEABLE.

DON'T LET ANYTHING COME BETWEEN YOU AND THE SUN. **BESIDES A NICE HELPING OF SUNSCREEN, THAT IS.**

HAVE A FIRM HANDSHAKE. **NO ONE IS IMPRESSED BY A LIMP, FLOPPY-FISH HANDSHAKE.**

GIVE A DOLLAR TO A STRANGER WHO NEEDS IT.

RETURN YOUR SHOPPING CART TO ITS PLACE.

HAVE A HAPPY PLAYLIST.

Sounds weird, but trust me. Having a playlist of songs that can cheer you up or lift your spirits is a pretty useful thing to have.

TEXTING AND WALKING SHOULD NEVER BE FRIENDS.

LOOK UP AND OUT AT WHAT'S GOING ON AROUND YOU.

UNPLUG YOURSELF. Phones and Internet and TV are great and all, but there's a peacefulness of sitting outside and listening to the wind blow through the trees you won't find in all the screens.

ALWAYS BE TRYING TO BETTER YOURSELF.

Alexander the Great supposedly cried because there were no more worlds to conquer. There is no peak you can reach, and if your reach always exceeds your grasp, you'll always have something to aspire to—a sense of forward movement.

TIP WELL.

EVERY DAY, DO AT LEAST ONE THING JUST FOR THE FUN OF IT.

SOMETIMES THE LITTLE THINGS IN LIFE MAKE THE BIGGEST DIFFERENCE. A LITTLE SMILE . . . A LITTLE PAT ON THE BACK . . . A LITTLE HELPING HAND.

DON'T BURN BRIDGES.

YOU MAY NEED A FAVOR OR A REFERENCE FROM THAT JACKASS SOME DAY.

DON'T MOW MORE THAN 1/3 OF THE GRASS HEIGHT OFF AT ONE TIME. UNLESS IT'S LIKE A JUNGLE OUT THERE.

PUNCTUALITY IS GREAT, but it's better to be late than to drive too fast. If you're behind schedule, take a deep breath and remind yourself that time is relative. Einstein said so, and he was a genius.

WEAR THESE THINGS EVERY DAY:

**KINDNESS, PATIENCE, COMPASSION, AND CLOTHES.
IN NO CERTAIN ORDER OF IMPORTANCE.**

FIND SOMETHING NEW TO GET EXCITED ABOUT.

A NEW TV SHOW, SPORT, HOBBY, BOOK, BAND, LIVE EVENT . . . OPPORTUNITY IS EVERYWHERE.

SHOW GRATITUDE.

Someone taking the time to do something kind or positive for you is a great gift. Make sure they know you appreciate it.

ENJOY THE POSSIBILITIES EACH DAY HAS TO OFFER. **THE THOUGHT ALONE OF COVERING THINGS IN CHEESE INSTANTLY PUTS YOU AHEAD OF THE GAME.**

KEEP YOUR TIRES INFLATED CORRECTLY AND GET YOUR OIL CHANGED WHEN IT'S TIME. DO THESE TWO SIMPLE THINGS, AND YOU'LL BE AMAZED HOW LONG YOUR CAR CAN STAY RUNNING.

RECYCLE.

THERE IS NO REASON NOT TO. IT TAKES VERY LITTLE EFFORT, AND NOTHING BUT GOOD THINGS CAN COME FROM IT.

HAVE AT LEAST ONE OUTFIT THAT MAKES YOU FEEL COMPLETELY CONFIDENT.

RECOGNIZE GREATNESS.

EVERY MORNING IN THE MIRROR IS ALWAYS A NICE PLACE TO START.

SOMETIMES THE WORDS YOU DON'T SAY ARE THE MOST IMPORTANT. DO YOURSELF PROUD, AND LET YOUR ACTIONS SPEAK FOR YOU.

THERE'S NO RIGHT WAY TO GO THROUGH LIFE.

Plenty of wrong ways, though. Luckily, you know the difference. If you find yourself doubting that, I'm always here.

JUST ONCE, CALL IN PERFECTLY HEALTHY.

SPEND YOUR DAY OFF DOING SOMETHING YOU LOVE.

A GUY NEEDS THREE FRIENDS: ONE WHO'LL KEEP HIM ON HIS TOES, ONE WHO'LL BOOST HIS EGO, AND ONE WHO'LL BE THERE NO MATTER WHAT.

CLEAN YOUR MICROWAVE.

Microwaves get gross. An easy cleaning tip is to microwave a bowl of water for about 6 minutes. The steam it creates helps loosen crusty food splatter, and then the hot water still in the bowl serves as a clean, chemical-free way to make your microwave shine.

GOOD TIMES MAY DASH PAST. TOUGH TIMES MAY CRAWL BY. THE MAIN THING IS TO **STAY IN THE RACE.**

CHECK YOUR FOUNDATION ONCE A YEAR.

....

LIFE IS IMPROVISATION.

WE'RE ALL FIGURING IT OUT AS WE GO.

....

GOOD THINGS COME TO THOSE WHO THINK NAPS AND RERUNS AND LEFTOVER PIZZA ARE BLESSINGS. See also: green lights during your commute, a dollar bill in your jeans pocket, indoor plumbing, holding hands in movies, and butterflies. Even a headache can be a blessing if you vow to be grateful when it stops.

YOUR FIRST HOUSE WON'T BE PERFECT.

It won't be as nice as you'd want it to be, and there might even be a few things that you don't like. But remember that it is **YOUR** home, and you can make it whatever you want it to be over time.

STRESS IS NORMAL, BUT DON'T OVERDO IT.

No matter how difficult or hard times might get, remember that life is a long road, and the potholes are few and far between.

EVERY NOW AND THEN, DO SOMETHING THAT MIGHT GO DOWN ON YOUR PERMANENT RECORD. BIG SECRET— there's no such thing as your "permanent record." So don't be afraid to take bold risks, as long as they put you forward in the direction you want to go.

HAVE A FAVORITE SPORTS TEAM.

PEOPLE > $$$. PEOPLE > THINGS. INVEST YOUR MONEY AND TIME AS SUCH.

HAVE A TOOLBOX WITH ALL THE ESSENTIALS. **KNOWING HOW TO USE THEM HELPS, TOO.**

THERE'S NOTHING LIKE FINDING THE RIGHT ONE TO GROW OLDER AND CRAZIER WITH. This is the epitome of true love, by the way. Keep looking 'til you find this person. Accept no substitutes. Forever is a long, long time. But if you're with the right person, it's not long enough.

EAT SOMETHING WEIRD EVERY ONCE IN A WHILE.

START SMALL, THEN WORK YOUR WAY UP TO THE CHICKEN-FRIED CAKE.

FIND A HOLE IN YOUR DAY WHERE AWESOME CAN DROP IN TO VISIT. SERVE IT SOMETHING COLD TO DRINK. ASK IT TO STAY AWHILE. I'M PRETTY SURE YOU TWO WILL HAVE LOTS IN COMMON.

OFFER YOUR DATE THE SEAT WITH THE BEST VIEW.

LOOK PEOPLE IN THE EYE WHEN YOU THANK THEM.

WIN SOME.
LOSE SOME.

GO DOWN IN GLORIOUS FLAMES SOME.

In other words, try. And if at first you don't succeed, keep trying your butt off. A no-fail life is a no-fun life. Make a big mistake every day and get it over with. Learn from it and move on.

BE KIND TO WAITERS. WAITING TABLES CAN BE HARD, EXHAUSTING WORK. AND YET WAITERS STILL DO THEIR BEST TO MAKE SURE YOU HAVE A POSITIVE EXPERIENCE WHEN EATING OUT. SO REMEMBER: SAY PLEASE, SAY THANK YOU, BE PATIENT, AND ALWAYS, ALWAYS TIP. YOU DON'T WANT SOMETHING EXTRA ENDING UP IN YOUR MEAL.

SETBACKS HAPPEN TO EVERYONE—IT'S HOW WE REACT THAT MAKES THE REAL WINNERS STAND OUT. IF YOU COULD BOTTLE "RESILIENCE" AND SELL IT, YOU'D NOT ONLY GET RICH, YOU'D BE HELPING THE WORLD IN A REAL GAME-CHANGING WAY.

HANG IN THERE.

HAVE FAITH THAT YOU'RE ON YOUR WAY TO BETTER DAYS.

YOU CAN WAIT FOR THE STORM TO PASS, OR YOU CAN GO OUT AND ENJOY THE RAIN. **Be like a duck to the puddles. Jump in feet first once in a while. Life's a quack-up. Don't worry about paying me for the advice. I'll put it on your bill.**

"BECAUSE I'M SMOKIN' HOT?" IS NOT THE CORRECT ANSWER TO "DO YOU KNOW WHY I PULLED YOU OVER?" ALWAYS REMEMBER—BOTH HANDS ON THE WHEEL AND MOUTH IN "PARK."

LET THINGS AMAZE YOU.

The world can be really boring if we let it be. Or, with the right perspective, it can be a beautiful place full of sights and sounds and experiences that show how incredible this world really is.

BE NICE TO YOUR FAMILY.

WE KNOW ALL YOUR SECRETS.

GO TO THE HARDWARE STORE AND HAVE THEM MAKE A COPY OF ALL THE IMPORTANT KEYS IN YOUR LIFE.

Give them all to someone you trust. Implicit in this advice is the importance of filling your life with people you trust. You could also wear the extra keys on a shoelace around your neck, though it's a little easier for kindergartners to rock that look.

LISTEN TO OLD PEOPLE'S STORIES.

WATCH YOUR LANGUAGE. The Founding Fathers fought for our free speech. Don't squander it on the f-word.

DON'T WATCH TOO MUCH CABLE NEWS. Keeping up to date on events is important, but remember that cable news channels are mostly concerned with ratings and tend to cater to certain demographics. With that in mind, always get your news from multiple sources, and try to find the truth that all of them agree on.

YOU'RE ON A MAJOR JOURNEY. PACK A GRANOLA BAR. It's the perfect sustenance—full of good energy, low maintenance, and just a little bit nutty. Which are also good qualities in friends, by the way.

TAKE A COMPLIMENT WHEN IT'S GIVEN TO YOU.

LIFE IS MULTIPLE CHOICE.

If you are here reading this, chances are you've made your share of good choices by now. Chances are you made some less fortunate ones, too, and I really don't need to know about those. Regret nothing. Learn from the "what was I thinking" disasters and turn them into shining moments.

NOT ALL YOUR GOALS HAVE TO BE BIG.

Nothing wrong with little goals you can achieve in a day. A sense of achievement is what keeps us going.

KEEP EMERGENCY SNACKS IN YOUR CAR.

THINK NON MELTY: NUTS, PRETZELS, CRACKERS, DRIED FRUIT, ETC.

THERE IS SUCH A THING AS TOO MUCH DETERGENT. And I'm not talking the funny, suds-all-over-the-floor-like-on-TV kind. If you open your washer after a cycle and your clothes are stiff and sticking to the sides of the machine, you're using too much.

YOU ARE ENOUGH.

NO OTHER PERSON SHOULD COMPLETE YOU, BECAUSE THERE IS NOTHING TO COMPLETE. THERE IS NO MISSING PIECE. JUST ONE COMPLETE, BEAUTIFUL MASTERPIECE THAT IS YOU. THIS IS COMPLETELY SELF-EXPLANATORY AND UTTERLY TRUE. THE IRONY IS THAT TRUE LOVE FINDS MOST PEOPLE WHEN THEY'RE MOST HAPPY WITH THEMSELVES AND COMFORTABLE BEING IN THEIR OWN COMPANY. I KNOW YOU. YOU'RE AWESOME. HOPE YOU KNOW AND BELIEVE IT.

ALWAYS BE LOOKING FORWARD TO SOMETHING. IT CAN BE SOMETHING AS BIG AS A NEW JOB OR SOMETHING AS SIMPLE AS A NEW MOVIE. BUT ALWAYS HAVE SOMETHING IN THE FUTURE THAT YOU'RE EXCITED ABOUT. IT WILL KEEP YOU ENERGIZED AND GET YOU THROUGH THE DULL PERIODS.

BE POSITIVE. Your brain continually rewires and forms new neuron paths to make certain pathways faster and more efficient. If you fill your mind with negative thoughts, it will become better at thinking negatively. So spend your time thinking about the good things in life: Positive is a much better default setting.

DON'T REPEAT MISTAKES.

MISTAKES HAPPEN, AND THEY SERVE A VALUABLE PURPOSE IN LIFE. USE THE LESSONS THAT YOU LEARN TO BETTER NAVIGATE YOUR NEXT LEARNING OPPORTUNITY.

CLEAN UP AFTER YOURSELF.

BEEHIVES MAKE LOUSY PIÑATAS. "POKING THE BEAR" MEANS PICKING A BIGGER FIGHT THAN YOU'RE PREPARED TO HANDLE. ASK BASICALLY ANY GENERAL WHO'S TRIED TO INVADE RUSSIA. SOMETIMES YOU'VE GOTTA COUNT THE COST BEFORE YOU THROW THE FIRST PUNCH.

ENJOY MOMENTS JUST FOR YOU.

PUT YOUR CELL PHONE AWAY AND ENJOY LIFE'S ADVENTURES. NO NEED TO TWEET ABOUT IT, TAKE A PICTURE, OR RECORD A VIDEO. JUST ENJOY THE EXPERIENCE.

MAKE THE MOST OF WHAT YOU ARE.

AND WHATEVER YOU ARE, BE A KICK-ASS ONE.

IT'S OK TO NOT BE OK.

AND IT'S OK TO ADMIT IT. AS MUCH AS PEOPLE LIKE TO TALK ABOUT THEIR PHYSICAL AILMENTS, MENTAL ILLNESS IS TREATED LIKE A TABOO SUBJECT. EVERYONE HAS BUMMER DAYS, AND EVERYONE HAS VULNERABILITIES. PLEASE UNDERSTAND THE IMPORTANCE OF YOUR MENTAL HEALTH.

STAND UP FOR THE WEAKEST GUY. **IT'LL MAKE YOU STRONGER.**

IF YOU'RE GONNA HAVE THE PIE, MIGHT AS WELL HAVE THE ICE CREAM, TOO. A little extra deliciousness once in a while is good for the soul. You're worth it. And I'm not just saying that because you're my son. For the record, though, you're a great son who deserves ice cream with his pie.

IT'S JUST A JOB. As of 2015, about sixty percent of college graduates work in a job outside their field of study. And it's fair to say that it's not their "dream job." But it's important to remember that happiness and fulfillment should not come solely from what you do for work. They should also come from all the fun and interesting experiences and hobbies you have outside of the workplace.

TAKE A BREAK.

YOU CAN GET BACK TO THE REAL WORLD LATER.

APPRECIATE WHAT YOU HAVE. GREEN GRASS. BLUE SKIES. WARM SUNSHINE. FRESH AIR. FEEL FREE TO KEEP THIS LIST GOING.

COUGH INTO YOUR ELBOW. It's amazing how this was only recently accepted as the norm. But do not cough into your hands. Yes, you didn't send projectile spit and phlegm everywhere. But now all that grossness is on your hands, which touch everything. This is why you should always cough into your elbow; it touches nothing and no one touches it.

NEVER GO TO BED ANGRY.

ALWAYS KEEP SOME FUNNY NOSE GLASSES ON HAND.

TAKE THEM OUT FOR A SPIN WHENEVER YOU FEEL YOURSELF TAKING LIFE TOO SERIOUSLY. BONUS POINTS IF YOU CARRY A SPARE FOR A FRIEND.

INVEST IN A HAMMOCK.

KEEP A LEVEL HEAD.

It's easy to be upset. But staying cool and calm when things get heated helps other people stay that way, too. In some cases, it makes them realize maybe things aren't as bad as they seem.

READ THE SMALL PRINT ON COUPONS.

TAKE TIME TO RECHARGE YOUR BATTERIES. **YOUR METAPHORICAL BATTERIES, NOT YOUR ACTUAL BATTERIES. PLEASE RECYCLE THOSE.**

THERE'S A WAY OUT OF EVERY PROBLEM.

Every issue you face, every dilemma you find yourself in, has a solution. You just have to be calm, clearheaded, and clever enough to see it. Or, at the very least, be able to know when it's time to call someone for help. You know the home number.

RUN A MARATHON. OR MAYBE JUST 26.2 SECONDS. EITHER WAY, YOU'LL BE BETTER FOR IT.

LITTLE-KNOWN FACT: EVERYTHING IS GUILT-FREE IF YOU QUIT WORRYING ABOUT IT. Guilt's an OK emotion. It's shame that's a killer. It's OK to feel bad for something you do—especially if you resolve to fix it—but never about who you are.

BE YOUR OWN HAPPY.

SOMEONE ELSE'S HAPPY WOULDN'T LOOK QUITE AS GOOD ON YOU.

SPOIL YOURSELF.

DON'T ENTERTAIN REGRETS.

THEY'RE THE SORT OF COMPANY THAT NEVER KNOWS WHEN TO ZIP IT SHUT AND LEAVE.

LIFE IS MUCH TOO SHORT TO WASTE TIME EXPECTING IT TO MAKE SENSE.

TREAT OTHERS HOW YOU WOULD LIKE TO BE TREATED.

All those feelings you feel—happiness, sadness, joy, embarrassment—are also felt by everyone else. So make sure you're never the reason someone feels the bad ones.

LIFE IS LIKE A RESTAURANT. DON'T ORDER MEAT LOAF AND EXPECT TO GET LOBSTER. If you don't have a vision for what you want in life, you'll be tempted to let too many days go by half-lived. Spend at least a minute each day thinking about the big picture. If you're a meat loaf kinda guy, make it the best meat loaf in the land. If you're more of a lobster kinda guy, get going on building the best traps.

....

DO SOMETHING TO YOUR BEST ABILITY THE FIRST TIME.

IF YOU INVEST THE TIME AND ENERGY INTO DOING IT RIGHT, YOU WON'T HAVE TO DO IT AGAIN LATER.

....

YOU CAN MAKE IT THROUGH A BUSINESS TRIP WITH FIVE SHIRTS AND ONE TIE.

....

WHEREVER YOU ARE ON THIS JOURNEY, YOU'RE RIGHT WHERE YOU'RE MEANT TO BE. The time we have—it's not a race. Live, love, and learn at your own pace.

ALWAYS TREAT TROUBLE LIKE IT'S TEMPORARY.

IT CAN'T OUTLAST THE GOOD THINGS IN LIFE.

PLAN A WEEKEND TRIP.

IT'S NOT GETTING UP MOUNT EVEREST THAT'S THE HARDEST—
IT'S GETTING DOWN. Climbers have to have the discipline to plan
their descent as meticulously as their ascent. It's no fun to plan
for the later part of your life, but if you live the first half right, the
second half will be more fun than you can even dream.

COUNT YOUR BLESSINGS, NOT YOUR PENNIES.

IT'S EASY TO CONFUSE THE TWO IN A WORLD THAT GLORIFIES
MONEY. BUT ALL THE CASH IN THE WORLD WON'T BUY YOU A
SUNRISE. AND EVEN THE MOST PRODUCTIVE INVESTMENT PORT-
FOLIO WON'T KEEP YOU WARM AT NIGHT. WORK HARD AND THANK
HARD. THAT'S THE SECRET TO EVERYTHING.

THE VERY BEST PLACE TO LIVE WILL
ALWAYS BE IN THE MOMENT.
**THERE'S A LOT TO BE THANKFUL FOR
IN THE HERE AND NOW.**

IT'S GOOD TO LOOK UP TO SOMEONE. IT'S NOT OK TO PUT THEM ON A PEDESTAL. **ONE WILL KEEP YOU INSPIRED AND MOTIVATED. THE OTHER WILL KEEP YOU SEEDED IN JEALOUSY.**

VOLUNTEER YOUR TIME.

BE CAREFUL WITH THE INTERNET.

Always ask yourself, "Would my folks be upset if I said this to them?" before clicking "Post." It's the simplest way to keep yourself from posting something you'll regret later.

HEED THE WORDS OF DAMON RUNYAN: "All horseplayers die broke." **In related news, at a casino, the house always wins. Gambling is risky. The only things that are sure bets are your imagination and determination. Oh, and a parent's love.**

SOME DAYS, YOU GET THE GOLD STAR.

SOME DAYS, YOU GET THE "YOU TRIED" STICKER. SOME DAYS, THERE'S NO STAR OR STICKER. There's just the comfort and pride of knowing you did your best. On those days, give yourself a sticker AND a star.

DRINK EIGHT GLASSES OF WATER A DAY.

NOT SODA. NOT JUICE. WATER. THE BENEFITS ARE IMMEASURABLE. SO THERE.

THERE'S A TIME AND A PLACE FOR EVERYTHING. ES-PECIALLY SWEARING. SOMETIMES THAT $#!% REALLY HELPS. SOMETIMES, THOUGH, YOU SHOULD PROBABLY JUST KEEP IT TO YOURSELF.

DRIVE FOR SHOW, PUTT FOR DOUGH.

Literally true when you're golfing. The metaphor holds true for other things, too. Paint the trim meticulously. Plate the food like the artist you are. The joy and magic is in the patient and lovely execution of the details.

TAKE THE BACK ROADS AND ENJOY THE SCENERY. FRONT ROADS ARE FOR AMATEURS AND ADVENTURE-PHOBES.

DON'T TAKE UP SEATS IN A CROWDED MOVIE THEATER.

MAKE TIME FOR BREAKFAST. Even if it's just one of those breakfast bars or protein drinks. Eating something first thing in the morning gives you the energy to get through the start of the day. It also helps with kick-starting your metabolism. (Not sure if you're too worried about that yet, but it's a good thing to remember.)

MEASURE TWICE, CUT ONCE.

WHEN CUTTING WOOD (OR ANYTHING, REALLY), MAKE SURE TO MEASURE TWICE TO ENSURE YOU HAVE THE RIGHT LENGTH, 'CAUSE ONCE YOU CUT, IT'S CUT.

ALWAYS OFFER YOUR SEAT TO SOMEONE WHO NEEDS IT MORE. THIS CAN BE AN ACTUAL SEAT OR A METAPHOR FOR SOMETHING SOMEONE ELSE NEEDS MORE THAN YOU.

WALK TO THE DOOR TO MEET YOUR DATE.

NO TEXTING FROM THE CAR. NO HONKING, EITHER.

TAKE A NEW ROUTE HOME.

CLEAR SKIES AND EASY ROADS DO NOT A WARRIOR MAKE. Don't get me wrong. Given the choice, I would wish you clear skies and easy roads, at least occasionally. But your motivation and your ability are forged stronger by gale-force winds and bumpy roads with gravel kicking up and scratching your fenders a little. But no human is entitled to a cushy ride. If it looks like someone has an easy ride, you can be sure there's a burden invisible to you that's making a warrior out of him or her, too.

••

INSTALL A GOOD ANTIVIRUS PROGRAM ON YOUR LAPTOP OR COMPUTER.

••

DO WHAT YOU NEED TO DO.

SIT-UPS. LAUNDRY. ABSOLUTELY NOTHING. TOTALLY YOUR CALL.

••

TRY TO LEARN TO SEW. EITHER YOU'LL BECOME A MASTER AT IT, AND YOU'LL HAVE LEARNED A VERY VALUABLE SKILL (OR AT LEAST HOW TO FIX A BUTTON), OR IT'LL BE REALLY HARD AND FRUSTRATING FOR YOU, IN WHICH CASE YOU'LL HAVE A DEEPER APPRECIATION FOR ALL THE LITTLE THINGS YOUR MOM HAS DONE FOR YOU.

> READ THE CLASSICS. AS YOU GET OLDER, THE TOPICS CLASSIC LITERATURE COVERS BECOME SO MUCH MORE RELATABLE. NOT TO MENTION CLASSICS ARE SOMETIMES SOLD IN COOL LEATHER-BOUND COPIES.

DON'T SMOKE.

SERIOUSLY. DON'T DO IT. IT'S A TRAP, AND I GUARANTEE THAT SOMEDAY YOU'LL WANT TO QUIT. YOU WON'T WANT ME STANDING THERE SAYING I TOLD YOU SO.

GET EXPERIENCE DRIVING DIFFERENT TYPES OF VEHICLES. Nothing wrong with driving an automatic, but be comfortable driving other vehicles, too. Rental vans, a manual, a big truck...each is different, and all could be useful at some point.

DO WHAT YOU LOVE.

This sounds easy, but lots of people don't do this. A good amount of our lives is spent working, so it's important to make sure you love what you do. Not to mention it'll make that time go so much quicker.

BUDGET YOUR MONEY.

Or at least be conscious of your spending habits. The big TV may seem like a necessity, but it's nice to be able to pay the bills and still have some money left over for the fun stuff.

SUCCESS ISN'T ALWAYS ABOUT THE END RESULT. Most times, it's about the people you made smile along the way.

HAPPINESS AND DAYLIGHT—NO MATTER WHAT, THEY ALWAYS COME BACK. AND NO MATTER WHAT, IF YOU NEED A REMINDER, I'M JUST THE PERSON TO PROVIDE IT. KEEP THE FAITH. IF IT SLIPS THROUGH YOUR FINGERS, CALL A FRIEND. OR ME. NO MATTER WHAT, I'M ON YOUR SIDE.

REACH OUT TO AN OLD FRIEND OR MENTOR.

DON'T TRY TO HIT A GOLF BALL FAR. It's more about form and control than just blindly powering through in your swing. The same can be said for life.

WASH YOUR WINDOWS EVERY TWO MONTHS.

LET THE SUNSHINE IN.

THERE'S NO WAY TO DO PERFECT, BUT THERE ARE ALL KINDS OF WAYS TO DO GOOD. Grand gestures and formal philanthropy are amazing for those who can manage them. But don't forget that a smile and some friendly eye contact can make the difference to that person on the bus or the exhausted parent at the store. We're all in this together, and the more we love, the more joy we feel.

KNOW AN EASY RECIPE OR TWO.

Even if you hate cooking, it's good to have one go-to recipe in case you need to bring a dish to a potluck or an event of some kind.

ONE SIMPLE RECIPE IS FOR BARBEQUE MEATBALLS:

- Fill a slow cooker with pre-cooked meatballs.
- Add enough barbecue sauce to cover all the meatballs (usually about two bottles).
- Turn the slow cooker to "warm." Let them simmer until the meatballs get soft and warm. Make sure to stir sporadically to ensure all the meatballs get covered.

USE A PHONE CASE.

IT'S A SMALL INVESTMENT THAT CAN SAVE YOU HUNDREDS.

LOVE WHO YOU LOVE.

LOVE THEM FIERCELY AND WITHOUT APOLOGIES.

NO "ADJUSTING" IN PUBLIC. T'S JUST NOT A CLASSY THING TO DO. BUT IF IT'S UNBEARABLE, AT LEAST TRY TO BE SUBTLE ABOUT IT.

TRY EVERYTHING ONCE.

A NEW SPORT, A WEIRD FOOD . . . YOU WON'T KNOW WHETHER IT'S YOUR THING UNLESS YOU TRY IT.

DON'T START EATING UNTIL EVERYONE AT THE TABLE HAS HIS OR HER FOOD. WAITING IS A SIGN OF RESPECT AND GOOD MANNERS. IT ALSO TELLS THE OTHER DINERS YOU VIEW THEM AS PEOPLE WORTH WAITING FOR.

NEVER RENT APPLIANCES.

THERE ARE MORE IMPORTANT THINGS TO MAKE BESIDES MONEY. Make: time, merry, do, sense, peace, room, waves, amends, pizza, believe, the most of the day that's been given to you.

KEEP AN EXTRA PACK OF AA AND AAA BATTERIES AROUND, AND A BOX OF LIGHT BULBS. THEY ALWAYS GO OUT AT PRECISELY THE TIME WHEN YOU NEED THEM MOST.

DON'T CHECK YOUR PHONE DURING A MOVIE OR NIGHT OUT.

IF IT'S AN EMERGENCY, POLITELY EXCUSE YOURSELF AND TAKE CARE OF THE SITUATION IN PRIVATE.

BE FRIENDS WITH ALL KINDS OF PEOPLE.

By being close with people who have had different life experiences than you have, you are taught a lot about just how wonderfully unique this world can be.

DON'T WORRY IF YOUR JOB SEEMS SMALL AND YOUR REWARDS SEEM ALL TOO FEW. When you're first starting out, you may have to prove yourself on a few crappy jobs to earn your stripes and win respect. But your skills and character will stand out and speak for you and open up all kinds of other opportunities.

EAT YOUR VEGGIES.

YEAH, YEAH, THIS IS ONE OF THOSE CLICHÉ PARENT THINGS TO SAY. BUT IT'S TRUE.

ALWAYS WALK WITH DETERMINATION. BEST OF ALL, IF YOU LOOK LIKE YOU KNOW WHERE YOU'RE GOING, OTHERS WILL FOLLOW YOU.

KNOW THE DIFFERENCE BETWEEN A REPUTABLE SOURCE AND GOSSIP. **WHEN TALKING WITH FRIENDS, WHILE ONLINE, AND WHILE WRITING ACADEMICALLY.**

HUG THE PEOPLE IN YOUR LIFE.

DARE TO SUCK AT SOMETHING. FAILURE IS A FRIEND WHO CAN TEACH YOU LOTS OF REALLY GREAT STUFF.

BUY A GOOD HEAVY-DUTY VACUUM. **One that can also suck up water. Seriously, when something spills or breaks or leaks, you can't put a price on the convenience of that bad boy waiting for you in the corner.**

DO THINGS YOU'VE NEVER DONE BEFORE.

You'll learn something new about yourself by doing so, and it'll also give you a deeper understanding and respect for those who can do it better.

STAY HUMBLE.

IT'S GOOD TO HAVE PRIDE IN YOURSELF, BUT IT'S EVEN HEALTHIER TO RECOGNIZE THAT THERE ARE STILL THINGS YOU DO NOT KNOW OR MIGHT NOT BE SO GREAT AT.

MEMORIZE YOUR EMERGENCY CONTACT'S PHONE NUMBER. **CELL PHONES ARE GREAT, BUT THEY HAVE A LIMITED BATTERY LIFE AND RANGE.**

SLEEP IN EVERY NOW AND THEN.

Not to be confused with being lazy. Sometimes, it's good to just spend a couple extra hours on the weekend to fill the gas tank up and recharge.

KNOW HOW TO JUMP-START A CAR.

IF YOU USE A CREDIT CARD, USE IT RESPONSIBLY. **Having a good credit score is an important part of growing up. You'll need it to sign a lease, get a loan, or establish a financial history. But if you're going to charge up thousands of dollars in debt, or you don't trust yourself to use the card responsibly, it's better not to use it.**

WATCH OUT FOR HIDDEN MEANINGS IN WHAT PEOPLE SAY. For instance, "Want me to drive?" usually means "You drive like a maniac!" There's one exception to this "hidden meanings" business: "Love you, Son!" means exactly what it says. Always will.

PACK MORE UNDERWEAR THAN YOU THINK YOU'LL NEED.

HAVE TWO FAVORITE MOVIES. One should be the movie you feel is just a great movie, i.e. the one you consider the best movie of all time. The other movie should be the one that you watch on a rainy or bad day—the one you can count on to cheer you up.

Don't ask what the world needs. Ask what makes you come alive, and go do it. Because what the world needs is people who have come alive.—HOWARD THURMAN You have a uniqueness to bring to this world that it desperately needs.

JUMP INTO EVERYTHING WITH LOVE AND PASSION.

If you have enjoyed this book or
it has touched your life in some way,
we would love to hear from you.

Please send your comments to:
Hallmark Book Feedback
P.O. Box 419034
Mail Drop 100
Kansas City, MO 64141

Or e-mail us at:
booknotes@hallmark.com